The Lost Book of Noah

By Noah

ISBN: 978-1-63118-624-0

Christian Apocrypha Series

Other Books in this Series and Related Titles

The Acts of the Apostle John by John (978-1-63118-622-6)

The Ascension of Isaiah by Isaiah (978-1-63118-620-2)

The Book of Wisdom of Solomon by King Solomon (978-1-63118-502-1)

The Apocalypse of Peter by Peter (978-1-63118-527-4)

The Gospel of the Nativity of Mary by St. Matthew (978-1-63118-448-2)

The Vision of Saint Paul the Apostle by Paul (978-1-63118-526-7)

Early Translation of the Acts of the Apostles by Luke (978-1-63118-521-2)

The Hymn of Jesus by G. R. S. Mead (978-1-63118-409-3)

Psalms of Solomon by King Solomon (978-1-63118-439-0)

The First and Second Gospels of the Infancy of Jesus Christ (978-1-63118-415-4)

The Book of Parables by Enoch (978-1-63118-429-1)

The Testament of Abraham by Abraham (978-1-63118-441-3)

The Lives of Adam and Eve by Moses (978-1-63118-414-7)

Fourth Book of Maccabees by Josephus (978-1-63118-562-5)

Book of the Watchers by Enoch (978-1-63118-615-8)

Lost Chapters of the Book of Daniel and Related Writings (978-1-63118-417-8)

The Testament of Moses by Moses (978-1-63118-440-6)

Testaments of the Twelve Patriarchs (978-1-63118-579-3)

The Acts of Saint Andrew by Andrew (978-1-63118-623-3)

The Odes of Solomon by King Solomon (978-1-63118-503-8)

The Book of Astronomical Secrets by Enoch (978-1-63118-443-7)

Audio Versions are also Available on Audible, Amazon and Apple

4

Table of Contents

SERIES INTRODUCTION

The Apocrypha are a loosely knit series of books, written by early vanguards of Christianity (covering the eras of both the old and new testaments), and which comprise somewhere between about a dozen to several hundred titles, depending on whom you ask and how that person defines "Apocrypha." A small selection of these can still be found included in the Catholic bible, while a majority of the books in question, were abandoned by church officials in the early centuries of Christianity. Many of these apocryphal books were originally considered canon by early followers of Christ, in the first four centuries following his birth. It wasn't until the meeting of the Council of Nicaea in 325, that Emperor Constantine and a group of roughly 300 church bishops, gathered together with the goal of defining, standardizing and unifying an otherwise splintering Christianity, that many of these writings ceased to be included in the newly established canon. Enjoy then, this book as an example, of just one of the many books of the Christian Apocrypha, and be sure to check out other titles in this series.

INTRODUCTION

The Book of Noah has long captured the imagination of scholars and theologians due to its attributed authorship to Noah, a central figure in the biblical narrative. Although the book has not survived independently, it has been partially preserved in the Ethiopic Book of Enoch, the Book of Jubilees, and the Dead Sea Scrolls among other pieces. These extant fragments and references allow us to piece together a fascinating exploration of Noah's life, his prophetic experiences, and the significant themes that permeate the narrative.

As a pivotal figure in the Bible, Noah is renowned for his righteousness and unwavering faith in God. In a world increasingly consumed by sin, his steadfast devotion to God's commandments set him apart from the wickedness that surrounded him. His unwavering commitment to living a righteous life earned him a special place in God's plan for humanity.

In the early years of Noah's life, he witnessed the moral decline of society and the rampant wickedness that had taken hold of the hearts of men. Despite the growing darkness, Noah remained steadfast in his faith and continued to walk with God, seeking His guidance and wisdom.

The Book of Noah delves deeper into this narrative, providing a more comprehensive account of Noah's life, his divine encounters, and the wisdom he imparts to future generations. As the story unfolds, we learn of Noah's intimate relationship with God, which is marked by direct communication and profound spiritual experiences. These divine encounters not only deepen Noah's faith, but they also serve as the foundation for the wisdom he seeks to share with his family and future generations.

One such divine encounter occurs when God reveals His plan to cleanse the earth of its wickedness by sending a cataclysmic flood. Entrusted with this knowledge, Noah is chosen by God to build the ark and preserve life on earth. This monumental task requires unwavering faith and obedience, as Noah faces ridicule and disbelief from those around him. Nevertheless, he remains steadfast in his mission, trusting in God's plan and the promise of a renewed world.

Throughout the construction of the ark, Noah continues to experience divine encounters, further strengthening his faith and resolve. He is guided by God in every step of the process, from the selection of materials to the gathering of animals that will be preserved on the ark. As the time for the flood approaches, Noah's divine encounters serve as a source of comfort and reassurance, reminding him that God is with him in this monumental endeavor.

As the floodwaters recede and life begins anew, Noah emerges as a figure of hope and wisdom for future generations. He imparts the lessons he has learned through his divine encounters and experiences, emphasizing the importance of faith, obedience, and righteousness in the eyes of God. His story serves as a testament to the power of unwavering faith and the transformative potential of divine encounters.

In the Book of Noah, we gain a richer understanding of this central biblical figure, his spiritual journey, and the wisdom he imparts to those who follow. Through his life and divine encounters, Noah's story serves as an enduring example of the power of faith and the importance of living a righteous life in a world that is often marked by darkness and sin.

The Book of Noah, like many ancient texts, has a complex history that has been shaped and influenced by various sources over time. This work, though not extant as a complete text, can be partially reconstructed through the study of fragments, clues and references found in other writings. By examining these pieces, scholars can gain insight into the religious and cultural milieu from which the Book of Noah emerged.

Among the most significant discoveries related to the Book of Noah are the fragments found among the Dead Sea Scrolls. These ancient manuscripts, which date back to the Second Temple period, provide invaluable information about the beliefs, practices, and textual traditions of the time. The fragments of the Book of Noah found within the scrolls offer a glimpse into the original narrative and the themes that were important to its authors.

In addition to the Dead Sea Scrolls, references to the Book of Noah can be found in other pseudepigraphal works, such as the Book of Enoch and the Book of Jubilees. These texts, which were also written during the Second Temple period, share a common interest in the figure of Noah and the events surrounding the flood. By examining the ways in which these texts refer to and incorporate the Book of Noah, scholars can better understand the relationship between these works and the broader religious and cultural context in which they were produced.

One of the challenges in reconstructing the Book of Noah is determining the various sources and influences that have contributed to its development. Some scholars have suggested that the work may have initially been composed as a collection of individual stories, which were later combined and expanded upon by different authors. This would account for the varying styles and themes found within the fragments and references to the Book of Noah.

Another possibility is that the Book of Noah evolved over time through a process of transmission and reinterpretation. As the stories of Noah were passed down from one generation to the next, new elements and interpretations may have been added, resulting in a text that reflects the beliefs and concerns of different periods and communities.

Despite the challenges in reconstructing the Book of Noah, the fragments and references that have been discovered provide valuable insight into the religious and cultural milieu from which it emerged. The themes of divine judgment, human wickedness, and the importance of righteous living resonate throughout these texts, reflecting the concerns and beliefs of the communities that produced and transmitted them.

As scholars continue to study the fragments and references to the Book of Noah, they can not only piece together the narrative of this ancient work but also gain a deeper understanding of the religious and cultural context in which it was written. In doing so, they can shed light on the enduring significance of Noah as a figure of faith, obedience, and divine favor in the biblical tradition.

Chapter 1: The Birth of Noah

1. In the days when wickedness spread across the land, Lamech, a descendant of Adam through the line of Seth, was a righteous man. He remained faithful to God amidst the corruption and sin that permeated the world around him.

2. Lamech was married to a virtuous woman, and together they prayed for a child who would continue their legacy of righteousness and help guide humanity back to the path of God.

3. The Lord heard their prayers and blessed them with a son, whom they named Noah. Even from birth, it was evident that Noah was unlike any other child. A divine light surrounded him, and his countenance shone with an otherworldly radiance.

4. As Noah grew, his parents began to notice more extraordinary characteristics in their son. He was wise beyond his years and displayed a deep understanding of the divine laws that governed the universe.

5. Noah's wisdom and righteousness attracted the attention of the heavenly host. Angels descended to Earth to instruct him further in the ways of God, revealing to him sacred knowledge and mysteries beyond human comprehension.

6. Lamech and his wife marveled at the divine favor bestowed upon their son and recognized the great purpose for which he was born. They nurtured Noah's spiritual growth, teaching him the importance of obedience to God and the consequences of straying from the divine path.

7. As Noah matured, the wickedness of humanity continued to grow, and the Earth became filled with violence and corruption. God, in His infinite wisdom, saw the need to cleanse the world and begin anew.

8. The Lord chose Noah, the righteous and faithful servant, to be the instrument of this divine plan. God entrusted Noah with the immense responsibility of preserving life on Earth in the face of an impending cataclysmic flood.

9. Thus, from the very beginning, the birth of Noah marked the dawn of a new era in human history – an era where righteousness would triumph over wickedness, and hope would be rekindled for generations to come.

Chapter 2: The Wisdom of Noah

1. As Noah grew into adulthood, his wisdom and understanding of God's divine laws deepened. He became a beacon of righteousness in a world steeped in wickedness and sin.

2. Guided by the divine teachings of the angels and the wisdom imparted to him by his parents, Noah sought to share his knowledge with others. He dedicated his life to guiding humanity back to the path of God and away from the perils of sin.

3. Noah's teachings emphasized the importance of obedience to God, as well as the virtues of humility, compassion, and integrity.

4. He urged his fellow human beings to forsake their sinful ways and embrace the light of God's truth.

5. Many who heard Noah's teachings were moved by his wisdom and his unwavering faith in God. They recognized the truth in his words and began to follow the path of righteousness.

6. These followers formed the first community of believers, united in their commitment to living a virtuous life.

7. However, there were those who remained obstinate in their sinful ways, dismissing Noah's teachings as the

ramblings of a madman. They continued to indulge in their wickedness, refusing to heed the warnings of the impending divine judgment.

8. Despite the resistance he faced, Noah remained steadfast in his mission to spread the message of God.

9. He understood the immense responsibility entrusted to him and the dire consequences that awaited those who did not turn from their sinful ways.

10. Noah's wisdom extended beyond spiritual matters. He was also a skilled builder and a visionary planner, with an innate understanding of the natural world. These talents would prove invaluable in the construction of the ark, a monumental task that would require divine guidance and human ingenuity.

11. Through the years, Noah continued to share his wisdom with his family and followers, instilling in them a deep reverence for God and a commitment to righteousness.

12. His teachings would serve as a guiding light in the dark days that lay ahead, as humanity faced the divine judgment of the great flood.

13. In this way, the wisdom of Noah became a testament to the power of faith, righteousness, and perseverance. His unwavering commitment to God's divine plan

would ensure the survival of humanity and lay the foundation for a new beginning, where the righteous would inherit the Earth.

Chapter 3: The Royal Messiah

1. As Noah's wisdom reached the corners of the earth, he came to know the secrets of all living beings.

2. It was revealed to him that a royal messiah would arise, a chosen one whose birth and the breath of his spirit would be ordained by God.

3. The messiah would possess remarkable physical attributes, including a birthmark of reddish color on his hair and the shape of a lentil on his face, signifying his divine origin.

4. Even in his youth, the messiah would demonstrate an extraordinary understanding and wisdom, surpassing that of the learned men of his time.

5. As the messiah grew older, he would become versed in the three sacred books, which would grant him unparalleled knowledge and insight into the mysteries of creation.

6. His wisdom would extend to all peoples, and he would know the secrets of all living things, guiding them toward righteousness and justice.

7. The messiah would attract wise seers and sages, who would journey from afar to seek his counsel and learn from his teachings.

8. In times of conflict, the messiah would bring forth counsel and prudence, uniting the people under his just and benevolent rule.

9. The designs of those who sought to harm the messiah would come to nothing, for he was the Elect of God, and his rule would be great and everlasting.

10. Under the messiah's guidance, the world would flourish, and the people would live in harmony, walking in the path of righteousness as they looked toward a bright and hopeful future.

.

Chapter 4: The Call to Build the Ark

1. As the wickedness of humanity grew and the earth became filled with corruption, the Lord observed the depravity of His creation and decided to cleanse the earth with a great flood.

2. The Lord, in His mercy, chose Noah, the righteous one, to preserve the remnants of humanity and the animals, so that life could begin anew after the destruction.

3. One day, as Noah prayed and sought the guidance of the Lord, a divine vision appeared before him, commanding him to build an ark, a massive vessel that would shelter the righteous from the impending flood.

4. The vision provided Noah with detailed instructions on the construction of the ark, including its dimensions, the materials to be used, and the manner in which it should be built.

5. Noah, heeding the divine command, set about constructing the massive vessel, enlisting the help of his sons and the few who still remained faithful to the Lord.

6. The construction of the ark was met with ridicule and scorn from the wicked, who mocked Noah and his

family, unable to comprehend the divine purpose behind their actions.

7. Undeterred by the taunts of the unbelievers, Noah and his family persevered in their labor, driven by their unwavering faith in the Lord and the knowledge that they were fulfilling His divine plan.

8. As the ark neared completion, Noah received another vision, instructing him to gather his family and the chosen animals, ensuring the preservation of life as the waters began to rise.

9. Noah diligently collected pairs of animals from all corners of the earth, leading them into the safety of the ark, as the first drops of rain began to fall.

10. As the floodwaters engulfed the earth, Noah, his family, and the animals remained secure within the ark, entrusted by the Lord to begin a new chapter in the history of humanity and the world.

Chapter 5: The Flood and the New Beginning

1. As the floodwaters covered the earth, the ark was lifted upon the waves, and the wicked who had mocked Noah and his family perished in the deluge.

2. Inside the ark, Noah, his family, and the animals were protected by the grace of the Lord, who had not abandoned them in their time of need.

3. For forty days and forty nights, the rains poured down upon the earth, and the waters continued to rise, submerging the highest mountains beneath their depths.

4. As the days turned into weeks, Noah and his family tended to the animals within the ark, providing them with food and care, as they patiently awaited the abatement of the floodwaters.

5. In time, the rains ceased, and the waters began to recede, yet the earth remained submerged, with no sign of land emerging from the depths.

6. Noah, guided by the Lord's wisdom, sent forth a raven from the ark to seek any signs of dry land, but the bird returned empty-handed, unable to find a place to rest its feet.

7. After several days, Noah sent forth a dove, which returned with an olive branch in its beak, signifying that the waters had receded enough for trees to grow once more.

8. Noah waited seven more days and released the dove once more, but this time, the bird did not return, indicating that it had found a place to dwell upon the earth.

9. The Lord spoke to Noah, instructing him to lead his family and the animals out of the ark, for the time had come to repopulate the earth and begin anew.

10. As Noah, his family, and the animals emerged from the ark, they beheld a world cleansed of wickedness and corruption, and they gave thanks to the Lord for His mercy and protection during the great flood.

Chapter 6: Parables and Wisdom from Noah's Life

1. Noah, the faithful servant of the Lord, gathered his family around him and began to share parables, saintly advice, and life lessons drawn from his experiences, so that they might learn and grow in their faith.

2. Noah spoke of the time before the flood when the world was filled with wickedness and corruption, and he imparted the lesson that, even in the midst of darkness, the Lord will always preserve a remnant of the faithful who walk in His ways.

3. He recounted the ridicule and scorn he and his family endured while building the ark, teaching his children the importance of unwavering faith in the face of adversity and the need to remain steadfast in obedience to the Lord's commandments.

4. Noah shared the story of the raven and the dove, drawing a parable from their search for dry land. He encouraged his family to be like the dove, gentle, persistent, and hopeful in their pursuit of the Lord's guidance, rather than like the raven, which could not find a place to rest.

5. He urged his family to remember the days within the ark, where they tended to the animals and relied on the Lord's provision, emphasizing the significance of patience, compassion, and gratitude in their lives.

6. Noah warned his descendants of the dangers of pride and arrogance, recounting how the fallen angels' desire for power and self-importance led to their downfall and the suffering of humanity.

7. He spoke of the importance of humility, urging his family to always acknowledge the Lord's wisdom and submit to His will, for it is through submission that one can truly be uplifted and guided by the divine.

8. Noah shared a parable about the planting of the first vineyard, teaching his children that the fruits of their labor could be a source of blessing and abundance, but also warning them of the potential for overindulgence and harm if not consumed with moderation and thankfulness.

9. He encouraged his descendants to seek knowledge, understanding, and wisdom, as these were the tools that would guide them in their lives and help them discern the Lord's will.

10. Finally, Noah reminded his family of the importance of leaving a legacy of faith and righteousness, so that future generations might walk in the ways of the Lord and be a light unto the world.

Chapter 7: Noah's Vision of the Future

1. One day, as Noah stood upon the earth, now fertile and renewed after the great flood, he lifted his eyes toward the heavens and contemplated what the future might hold for him, his family, and their descendants.

2. As he gazed into the skies, the Lord granted Noah a vision, revealing glimpses of what was to come, both the blessings and the challenges that awaited the generations that would follow.

3. Noah saw the earth divided among his sons - Shem, Ham, and Japheth - each establishing their own lands and people, spreading far and wide across the face of the earth.

4. In the vision, he saw great cities rise from the ground, filled with people who would create wondrous inventions, harnessing the power of nature and discovering new ways to improve their lives.

5. Noah was shown a time when nations would come together to share knowledge, trade, and form alliances, fostering peace and unity among the people of the earth.

6. Yet, as the vision unfolded, Noah also saw the darker side of humanity's future. There would be wars and

conflicts, as people succumbed to greed, hatred, and the lust for power.

7. The vision revealed to Noah that his descendants would face times of hardship and persecution, testing their faith and resolve, and he saw that some would turn away from the path of righteousness, forgetting the lessons of the past.

8. In these moments of darkness, the Lord would raise up prophets and messengers to guide the people back to the truth, reminding them of the promises made to Noah and the enduring love of their Creator.

9. Noah saw that, through the generations, the Lord would continue to call upon the righteous to serve as beacons of light in a world often clouded by darkness, inspiring hope and faith in those who sought the truth.

10. And, as the vision faded, Noah was left with a sense of awe and humility, grateful for the Lord's guidance and the opportunity to bear witness to the unfolding story of creation.

Chapter 8: Noah's Glimpse of Heaven

1. As Noah's days on earth increased, and he continued to walk faithfully with the Lord, his thoughts turned to the eternal realm and the life that awaited him and his loved ones beyond this earthly existence.

2. One night, as Noah lay in his dwelling, the Lord granted him a wondrous vision of Heaven, the celestial abode where His divine presence dwelt in perfect harmony.

3. In the vision, Noah beheld a realm of unimaginable beauty, with radiant light that outshone the sun, and colors more vibrant than any he had ever seen on earth.

4. He saw the Garden of Eden, restored to its original glory, with the Tree of Life at its center, bearing fruit that imparted eternal life to all who partook of it.

5. Noah witnessed the host of angels who worshiped the Lord in unceasing adoration, their voices joined in harmonious songs of praise that filled the heavenly realm with melodies sweeter than any earthly music.

6. He saw the souls of the righteous who had departed from the earth, rejoicing in their eternal rest, reunited with their loved ones, and free from the pain and suffering of their mortal existence.

7. The vision revealed to Noah the divine throne, encircled by seraphim and cherubim, and upon it sat the Lord, in all His majesty and splendor, His countenance radiating love and mercy.

8. In the presence of the Almighty, Noah saw the saints and prophets of old, who, having fulfilled their earthly missions, now served the Lord in His heavenly kingdom, their wisdom and counsel valued and cherished.

9. As the vision unfolded, Noah was filled with a profound sense of peace, knowing that the Lord's promises would be fulfilled, and that Heaven awaited those who remained faithful and obedient to His commandments.

10. With renewed strength and determination, Noah carried the memory of the heavenly vision in his heart, sharing it with his family and descendants, that they too might draw hope and inspiration from the divine promise of eternal life.

EPILOGUE:
An Analysis of the Themes in The Book of Noah

The Book of Noah, as presented in the preceding chapters, offers a rich tapestry of themes that hold significant value for understanding the life and experiences of Noah as a prophet and his teachings.

A recurring theme in the Book of Noah is the significance of divine revelation and the role of prophecy. Noah is depicted as a chosen servant of God, receiving divine guidance and visions that reveal critical insights into the future. These revelations serve as a testament to Noah's unique relationship with the divine and his role as a mediator between God and humanity.

Noah's unwavering obedience and faith in God is another central theme in the book. As the narrative unfolds, Noah is seen following God's commandments, even when faced with seemingly insurmountable challenges. This theme highlights the importance of trust in divine guidance and the value of maintaining a strong connection with God, even in times of hardship.

The importance of righteousness in the eyes of God is emphasized in the Book of Noah. As a righteous man, Noah is chosen to preserve the human race and to act as a beacon of hope and guidance for future generations. This theme underscores the significance of living a life in accordance with God's will and maintaining a sense of moral integrity.

Throughout the narrative, the consequences of sin and disobedience are depicted in vivid detail. From the corruption of the earth by fallen angels to the cataclysmic flood, the Book of Noah serves as a cautionary tale, highlighting the consequences of turning away from God's commandments.

The themes of divine judgment and mercy are interwoven throughout the narrative. The flood serves as an example of God's judgment upon the wickedness that had overtaken the world, while the preservation of Noah and his family signifies God's mercy towards the righteous. This duality highlights the complex nature of the divine, embodying both justice and compassion.

The Book of Noah emphasizes the importance of passing down wisdom and life lessons to future generations. Through parables, saintly advice, and recounting the stories of his life, Noah seeks to instill in his descendants the values and principles that he has learned from his experiences and his relationship with God.

In short, the Book of Noah presents a multi-layered narrative that explores the life of a significant biblical figure, delving into themes such as divine revelation, obedience, righteousness, sin, judgment, mercy, and the importance of legacy and ultimately adds depth to our understanding of biblical narratives and the complex relationship between humanity and the divine.

www.ingramcontent.com/pod-product-compliance
Lightning Source LLC
LaVergne TN
LVHW091322080426
835510LV00007B/609